MW01089421

I-DJ

Gregg Barrios' *I-DJ* is a singular cultural mash-up. Using the indie label A&M Records, as well as Shakespeare's Hamlet, as reference points, the play chronicles the life of a gay Mexican-American DJ, who rechristens himself Warren Peace. While the music of the Tijuana Brass, the Carpenters, Peter Frampton and the Sex Pistols, forms a soundtrack, Warren spins his narrative odyssey from the tumultuous sixties to the LA club scene of the 1980s and the beginnings of the AIDS crisis. Barrios melds Chicano, LGBT and LA history into an original, witty and deeply moving play.

—Jeff Lunden, *NPR*

Packed with ecstatic beats from the 1980s A&M Records portfolio—and inspired by the narratives of *A Chorus Line* and *Hamlet*—playwright Gregg Barrios merges '70s Chicano politics with AIDS-era club culture to tell the story of queer DJ Amado Guerrero Paz (aka Warren Peace). Old school dance floor attitude meets the new dub-step style, when a younger DJ challenges Peace to a winner-takes-all musical standoff.

—*East Villager*

Saw my first four FRIGID New York shows today. The best production of the day was *I-DJ*, the story of a gay Mexican-American DJ from his childhood through the AIDS crisis, using the music of A&M Records. Amazing story, direction, and acting.

—Byrne Harrison, *Stage Buzz*

I-DJ is a runaway streetcar of emotion, poetry, and history, helmed by the indomitable Rick Sanchez. Telling the story of Warren Peace, the dynamic language and extreme circumstances of Warren's wild life surprise, move, and discomfit. This is not my first encounter with Gregg Barrios' work, and I was glad to see the continuing authenticity of his voice. It's a wonderful piece to see if you are interested in immersing in a slice of Stonewall era GLBT history with a Chicano lens.

—Joseph Samuel Wright, *The Easy*

In this world premiere play, Gregg Barrios takes us on a journey of one man who searches for validation as a Chicano and as a Dance Club DJ. Both coincide with his coming out. In part a one man show, the piece also features dancers, dance club music throughout the decades, a live DJ, video projections and a set by renowned graffiti artist Supher. Alternatively hilarious, devastating, and uplifting, this show is the perfect opening for the new Gregg Barrios Theater at The Overtime.

—*Broadwayworld.com*

In Gregg Barrios' wonderful *I-DJ* a character says, "It takes a fairy to make something pretty." And this play is it; a bejeweled handbag bursting to the seams with so much love for its place, passion for its music, and genuine care for its characters. A very pretty thing indeed!

—David Crabb, actor, playwright, memoirist of *Bad Kid*

The electrifying playlist in *I-DJ* pays high tribute to the 20th-century political histories of queer Chicano identity. Scored by a dazzling range from disco to techno, Gregg Barrios shows us that no story comes without its songs and no journey thrives without its anthems. *I-DJ* delivers an extraordinary musical performance!

—Rigoberto González, author of *Unpeopled Eden*

In *I-DJ*, a young man is given a Herb Alpert & the Tijuana Brass album and believes he has discovered the Latino role model he has been searching for. The play, which goes through the present day, takes in the turmoil of the times, digging into the civil rights movement, the struggle for gay identity, the AIDS crisis and other headline generators.

—Weekender 24/7
San Antonio Express-News

I-DJ continues and expands upon Gregg Barrios' reconstruction of American literary and cultural history by re-centering the trials and tribulations of a queer Chicano who resists homophobia and racism to become the omniscient narrator of one of the nation's most turbulent and creative eras, spanning the Vietnam War to the rise of another war in the 1980s: HIV/AIDS.

—*Q SanAntonio.com*

I-DJ

Other Works by Gregg Barrios

Drama

Rancho Pancho (2009)

I-DJ (2016)

Poetry

La Causa (2010)

Puro Rollo (1982)

Healthy Self (1979)

The Air-Conditioned Apollo (1979)

I-DJ

GREGG BARRIOS

HANSEN PUBLISHING GROUP, LLC

ISBN (trade paper) 978-1-60182-327-4
ISBN (ebook) 978-1-60182-328-1

Cover and book interior design by Jon Hansen

An earlier excerpt of *I-DJ* appeared in *Ollantay Theater Magazine*.

Author photograph by Bryan Rindfuss

Hansen Publishing Group, LLC
302 Ryders Lane
East Brunswick, NJ 08816

http://hansenpublishing.com

To The Fallen, The Caregivers, The Artists, The Beloved

Mickey Troncale • Charles Pierce • Danny Lozano • Larry Kert Rock Hudson • Freddie Mercury • Eloy Gomez • Joe Sanchez Derek Jarman • Paul Jabara • Felix Baragan • Greg Clayton Tina Chow • Mike Kelley • Drew Allen • Tony Richardson Hap Veltman • Brad Davis • Steve Rubell • Hibiscus • Liberace Howard Rollins • Cleo Tamez • Jacques Demy • Hector Lavoe Perry Ellis • Arthur Ashe • Jobriath • Salvador Rios Franco Marlon Riggs • Joseph Vasquez • Gil Scott-Heron • Easy-E Casey Donovan • Dan Hartman • David Fox • Ryan White Andy Bell • Phillip Roy Stansbury • Peter Allen • Herb Ritt Pedro Zamora • Alvin Ailey • Craig Russell • Tom Eyen Dorian Cory • Jason Payne • Esteban De Jesús • Joel Solis Malcolm Mclaren • Elizabeth Taylor • Colin Higgins Rudolf Nureyev • James Koss • Michel Foucault • Rollerena Leigh Bowery • Bruce Chatwin • Angie Xtravaganza James Merrill • Keith Haring • Leonard Matlovich • Fela Michael Bennett • John Boswell • Jack Smith • Randy Shilts Charles Ludlam • Harold Brodkey • Susan Sontag James Kirkwood • Howard Ashman • Lance Loud • Way Bandy Leonard Frey • Paul Monette • Néstor Almendros • Falco Mario Amaya • Robert Mapplethorpe •Wayland Flowers Carlos Almaraz • Willi Ninja • Sylvester • Warren Sonbert Joey Stefano • Homer Holguin • Gino Piserchio • Brad Davis Sterling Houston • James Wahl • Vito Russo • Pedro Cuevas Jorge Licón • Ricky Garcia • David Wojnarowicz • Halston Robert Joffrey • Reinaldo Arenas • Elton John • Magic Johnson Tony Kushner • Larry Kramer • Sylvia Rae Rivera • Nigel Finch Anthony Perkins • Gary Abrahams • Gary Essert • Jason Payne Stephen Harvey • Bill Sherwood • Howard Ashman • Al Parker Denholm Elliott • Scott Mcpherson • Kenneth Nelson • Dondi Robert La Tourneaux • Frederick Combs • Greg Louganis Terrence Mcnally • Cyril Collard • Elizabeth Glaser Isaac Asimov • Amanda Blake • David Alan Reis • Sam Wagstaff Ray Sharkey Jr. • Eric Baretto • Klaus Nomi • Mart Crowley

We won't die secret deaths anymore. The world only spins forward. We will be citizens. The time has come.

—Tony Kushner, *Angels in America*

CONTENTS

DOING *I-DJ*

Upon first meeting the loquacious and unguarded force of nature that is Warren Peace, you may be reminded of a chance encounter long ago on a bus, in a train station, or a public park — an unanticipated meeting with some bedraggled oracular *tipo*, who despite your clearly expressed discomfort at ceaseless over-sharing of unseemly details of his or her personal life, nonetheless leaves you shaken and changed.

Warren, born Amado Guerrero Paz, Gregg Barrios' indelible creation in *I-DJ* is such an entity, anointed as part street-side *joto* prophet, part reality show superstar (before there were reality shows), part arcane pop music archivist, daring his audience to keep up with him as he riffs through a rapid-fire Hegelian mash-up of his life *testimonio*, decades of recent social history, and the parallel hit list of the monster tunes that tracked and illuminated the whole story as it happened.

It's a bravura roller-coaster performance, joined *in medias res.*

As Master Peace expounds in his rather formal, stentorian in-vocation, "Tonight's ground rules are simple. Play original A&M Record vinyl releases — Nada más."

What follows will stagger you with a story that is at once deeply familiar, nothing but the hits, in the voice of Casey Kasem, and deeply disruptive, voicing a queering chronicle that might've been scripted by Michel Foucault, if he'd been a hustling Chicano raconteur DJ thespian channeling Shakespeare on Molly.

You see, Warren, too, has been shaped by his chance encoun-ters.

With Herb Alpert, *Mister Simpático*, pressing records in Warren's uncle's garage. An historic appearance on the David Susskind show. His first love, the *gavilán* Valentin, in the wash-room of the Gold Cup on Hollywood Boulevard, who'll soon come to an untimely end. His great love, the ethnomusicologist Kevin, who will come to his own untimely end.

Oh, untimely death.

Death slowly becomes the disco beat pulse that has syncopated our hero Warren's life, a rhythmic widening gyre that gradually takes up much of recent American history in its fatal embrace.

And the hits just keep coming, like a high school prom in a broke-down *razcuache* heaven. Herb Alpert & Tijuana Brass, *The Lonely Bull* and *Whipped Cream*. Carpenters, *Yesterday Once More* and *One Fine Day* and *Fun, Fun, Fun*. Chris Montez, *Call Me*. Cat Stevens, *Peace Train*. Procol Harum, *Conquistador*. Humble Pie, *I Don't Need a Doctor*. And on and on.

Only A&M ever, of course, *por favór*.

Even after we learn A&M's cofounder Herb Alpert isn't Mexicano—he's Armenian. But of course, Armenians are the Mexicanos of Mesopotamia, so it all just makes sense, funky Akashic sense.

Warren's discursive chops reveal just how profoundly pop music isn't just the sound track of our lives. It's the symphonic accompaniment to the inescapable zeitgeist of our being. Who keeps count of the number of funerals where *The Lonely Bull* has been piped through the speakers?

But Warren fearlessly leads us through the bildungsroman that has been his life, a series of awakenings, wounds and epiphanies that somehow make the world less estranged, less forbidding, murderous and oppressive. And even Michael Stipe must stand in wonder at this *vato's* volcanic capacity for name-checking history and the cavalcade of hits.

Commencing in the heart-piercing truth of popular song, Warren's story encompasses Chicano *conscientizacíon* and critiques of the *movimiento*, coming out, club culture ecstatic, eyes wide open witness to the devastating onset of AIDS. Warren Peace queers canons with a startling swagger, from American history to pop music, from machismo to gender illusionism.

Like all those chance encounters of our past, Warren Peace comes before you so that you might never forget his story. It's a kind of *compromise*.

At our parting, what seemed a random moment of fleeting human contact suddenly seems fated. Amidst the cascading litanies and hair-raising *cuentos*, something profound has been revealed.

As it always happens in sublunary world, *in medias res* renders us all to *memento mori*.

—John Phillip Santos

John Phillip Santos is the author of *Places Left Unfinished at the Time of Creation*, a finalist for the National Book Award. He is a University Distinguished Scholar in Mestizo Cultural Studies at the University of Texas, San Antonio.

FROM THE PLAYWRIGHT

The idea and the research for *I-DJ* came from those heady times of living and loving in Los Angeles from 1980 to 2000. It was one of the best rides of my life.

It would not have been possible without the late Irv Letofsky at the *LA Times* who taught me to write journalism with finesse. Ditto my creative writing teacher John Rechy. To the vinyl mavens at Tower Records; the theme night DJs Joseph Brooks and Henry Peck at Club Lingerie and Vinyl Fetish; the Sunset Strip, Aaron's Records on Melrose, and the folks at A&M Records especially Herb Alpert for his thumbs up and permission for the music. I extend my eternal gratitude to all the great artists on A&M.

I'd also be remiss not to mention my two-year fellowship at the Center Theater Group/Mark Taper Forum—especially Gordon Davidson, Diane Rodriguez and Luis Alfaro. Actor and director Danny De La Paz offered unconditional support when the play was a one-act about Jeffrey Hunter. He later played the lead at a staged reading for the Macondo Foundation. His wisdom and kindness gave me the fortitude to see this play into a full production.

I am most grateful to the Alfredo Cisneros del Moral Foundation for the commission I received to write this play and to Sandra Cisneros and the Macondo Foundation for their generous support.

For the San Antonio production, a big bear hug to the indefatigable Matthew Byron Cassi, a playwright's best man. I offer a big theatrical bow to The Overtime's Rob Barron and Kyle Gillette. And most importantly, the talented cast of *I-DJ*, Dominique Tijerina as the younger DJ and the superb Rick Sanchez, who won a local ATAC Golden Globe for his powerhouse performance as Amado-Warren.

For the Frigid Fringe production in New York City, I owe a debt of gratitude to Greg Hinojosa who under deadline pressure worked his magic in the "unplugged" version of *I-DJ*. Ditto to Rick Sanchez who reprised his role and won the hearts of the critics, and to Hunter Wolff for making his role as the young DJ his own. And a special nod to the folks at Frigid Fringe and UNDER St. Mark's for making my New York debut all I imagined it could be.

I offer a big shout-out to my publishers Jon and Jody Hansen. Their peerless imagining of the book from page to cover allows my work to shine in its best light.

Finally, I am humbled and honored that the main stage at the Overtime Theater Company bears my name. I remain confident that it will provide years—even decades of good, edgy, comic, dramatic and ridiculous theater from the wide diversity of talent in this city. The Overtime is the template for a new direction in theater for the twenty-first century. Mil gracias for letting my work be a small part of it.

PRODUCTION HISTORY

I-DJ opened at The Gregg Barrios Theater @ The Overtime in San Antonio, TX, July 13, 2012. Overtime Theater produced it. Matthew Byron Cassi was the director and the set and costume designer. Supher created the graffiti art. Sound and video design by Gregg Barrios and Matthew Bryan Cassi. Sophie Bolles was the stage manager. The cast was as follows:

RICK SANCHEZ   AMADO GUERRERO PAZ /
                                DJ WARREN PEACE

DOMINIQUE J. TIJERINA   DJ SILENCE / DJ MUTANT

*

The Woodlawn Theater and The Overtime Theater subsequently produced *I-DJ* in association with Frigid Fringe New York at Below St. Mark's Theater in New York City, NY as part of the 2014 Frigid Fringe Festival, February 19, 2014. Greg Hinojosa was the director and the set and costume designer. Sound design was by Gregg Barrios and Greg Hinojosa. The NY cast was as follows:

RICK SANCHEZ   AMADO GUERRERO PAZ /
                                DJ WARREN PEACE

HUNTER WULFF   DJ SILENCE / DJ MUTANT

Rick Sanchez as Warren Peace. Photograph courtesy of Matthew Byron Cassi.

I-DJ

The Odyssey dance club. Photographer Leo Jarzomb. Courtesy of the Los Angeles Public Library Photo Collection.

ACT ONE, SCENE ONE

Stage is dark. MUSIC fades in.

Lights come up on stage left behind DJ in silhouette at turntable.

(FAITHLESS, *GOD IS A DJ*)

DJ signs as the vocal begins.

DJ: (signing) "This is my church. This is where I heal my hurt...for tonight, God is a DJ."

Lights fade and come up on stage right platform.

WARREN enters. He is skating on the streets of Hollywood.

Slides and video chart his progress. He is dressed in black tights, white muscle Tee. He wears white face makeup. A DJ record tote over his right shoulder.

(DAVID BOWIE, *D.J.*)

WARREN: (singing) "I am a DJ, I am what I play, I got believers, believing me, oh!"

He removes his earbuds. Music out.

I just got cast in *Ham-a-lot*, a gay version of *Hamlet*.

To celebrate my successful casting, I naturally glided to Aaron's Records on Highland.

Eureka! A mother lode of pure virgin vinyl!

My day job? If you haven't guessed—the midnight shift at the Pair-A-Dice Ballroom in the heart of Hollywood.

I'm a DANCE CLUB queen. A Dee Jay DIVA!!

3

He stretches his arms into a flying robot pose and then moves his hands as if vogue dancing.

BLACKOUT

WARREN enters the Pair-a-Dice Ballroom. The backstage area abuts the club's DJ booth proper. There is also a couch, a TV set and a vanity.

WARREN places his tote on the couch, sits and removes his skates.

DJ, a young man in his twenties, stands behind the club turntables cueing disks.

DJ cues a classical fanfare.

(MEDIEVAL FANFARE)

WARREN: "You would play upon me, you would seem to know my stops, you would pluck out the heart of my mystery; you would sound me from my lowest note to the top of my compass; and there is much music, excellent voice, in this little organ; yet cannot you make it speak."

DJ looks quizzically at WARREN.

Don't look at me like that.

(turning to audience) Weren't you expecting Shakesqueer?

(to DJ) I got the part! Was that ever in question?

(gaily) "Go, make you ready."

WARREN sits at the dresser and drinks from bottled water.

Actually, I got the idea months ago from—are you ready?—Terrance McNally. We were pissing in the men's room of this very club!

"Warren, the greatest gay character is Hamlet. One of the reasons no one suspects he's gay is that he keeps his clothes on. When was the last time you saw a Hamlet who loosened his codpiece?"

WARREN glances at his crotch and readjusts his fanny pack.

As I zipped up, I endeared myself to the master class dramatist by offering my own bit of whimsy:

"Hamlet directs a play within the play. He's a goddamn director! Now, if that doesn't tell you he's gay—nothing will!"

(nostalgic) That was the night that Terrence blew me—A KISS.

WARREN digs through his DJ bag, and proffers a disk.

He sniffs and licks at the vinyl then shows his prized find to the audience.

Ah, the sweet smell of Licorice Pizza in the AM. What better way to start the day?

It's one of those picture disks from the Seventies. Oh, Peter Frampton was quite a beauty. *Frampton Comes Alive.* So did I. I was *way* out by then.

On any other night, this might be the perfect centerpiece for a fantastic show. But tonight is the anniversary of the closing of A&M Records.

Never heard of it?

OH, if some wise ass hollers out an Aggie joke, ignore the cowpoke, it isn't that kind of A&M.

He snaps his fingers.

SLIDES of A&M Record label and its offices in the old Charlie Chaplin Studios on Sunset Blvd.

The label's acronym comes from its founders: Herb Alpert and Jerry Moss. It was the last independent label to succumb to the corporate conglomerates. Its passing is still lamented in a town where fifteen minutes is an eternity.

Tonight's ground rules are simple. Play original A&M Record vinyl releases—*Nada más*.

Junior, back there is cueing a selection from the A&M catalog.

To raise the ante, if he cues a dozen cuts on my play list, then he fills in for a fortnight while I star in a gay one-man send-up of the immortal bard's most telling work at Outfest.

If HE veers from that, he's skating—

Motions to DJ's skateboard.

—On thin ice.

Well, he has yet to prove his mettle. He's begun badly.

(sniffing the air) I know the smell of my Gauloises!

Still, he learns fast, but he's forgetful. What can you expect? He's ADD, bipolar, tongue-tied, etc. etc. etc. What's going on with him isn't exactly clear. Even to me.

Yet I'm having jitters about tonight's special tribute.

A&M Records—was—IS the fucking soundtrack of my LIFE!

(HERB ALPERT & TIJUANA BRASS, *THE LONELY BULL*)

That was me all right: The lonely steer. It was hard for this seven-year-old Puck growing up in Whittier in 1963, the year of—"John F. Kennedy and The Beatles." Ah, birth place of Tricky Dick and Little Me. Oh god, I was witless in Whittier.

Alas, I soon learned I was Mexican, so I shouldn't get my hopes up too high. Not to worry, I discovered an aunt—mom's younger twin sister Luisa.

One afternoon, we left the tree-lined canopy of Whittier to visit Tía Luisa and her hubby Irv in West Hollywood.

When we got to 419 Westbourne, a gorgeous Latino beefcake came to the door. He didn't know where Irv and Tía lived. Westwood, perhaps?

Unbeknownst to us, Irv had rented the bungalow to Señor Simpatico and his business partner. They were pressing records in the garage!

Returning home, my father kept cursing about how much gas we'd wasted at 25 cents a gallon. Real big spender. My mother complained about his complaining.

I just gawked out the back window, knowing I'd live there someday among the beautiful people.

Weeks later, Tina Louise—oops, Tía Luisa drove out to Whittier in a brand new Cadillac El Dorado with fins all the way to Pico Rivera. She said she had a dream in the middle of the night—a dream that involved ME.

"Collect anything but collect." That was her—our mantra. Before I could ask what, Irv handed me a mint copy of the first A&M album, *The Lonely Bull*.

(shocked) Mister Simpatico was Herb Alpert!

WARREN strikes The Lonely Bull *LP pose.*

(HERB ALPERT & TIJUANA BRASS, *WHIPPED CREAM*)

Shows The Whipped Cream *album.*

I swear every family, in the East—I mean the Eastern part of LA—bought this fucking album. I took it as a sign of hope for our people.

I later heard the sexy, brown-eyed, brown-haired girl was three months pregnant when she posed for the cover. She had to be Mexican, right?

Wrong! Swedish. And that wasn't Cool Whip, it was shaving cream.

He shakes an imaginary container. And begins to shave for the first time.

He uses an Alpert LP image as a mirror.

Of course, I didn't have sideburns to trim yet. I wanted to look like Herb Alpert, my boyhood role model of a successful Latino.

But then Uncle Irv took me aside and explained the facts of life about the biz: "Alpert is a good Armenian Jew. But you couldn't do better than admire his chutzpah."

And I did. I brought my Herb Alpert and the Tijuana Brass record collection to school for show and tell. I already liked all eyes on ME. Afterward, my more macho classmates actually spoke to me.

My teacher was so impressed; she asked me to audition for a little theater production of *The King and I*.

I got the part a young Sal Mineo did on Broadway. Unbelievable! Etcetera, etc., etc.

My old lady told all her back fence comrades who oohing and aahing cooed: "*Amado es tan talentoso…y tan joto!*"

It isn't fathers who teach sons about MACHISMO. It's mothers. All through childhood, it was:

"Amado, don't touch your pee-pee"

Followed by — "Did you wash it, mijo?"

When anyone taunted me, she'd force me into a Mexican standoff.

"Well, little men don't do that! Go beat the shit out of that *cabrón*."

She spoon-fed me that with my Gerber's atole. She played her part to the hilt. A desperate housewife, who made enchiladas with Cheez-Whiz. Yuck-a-mole!

My old man wasn't much help. He stayed out of her way and expected me to follow in his staggering (belches) footsteps. He drank on weekends and beat the old lady with regularity.

Boy, could she take it. He'd leave her green eyes black and blue. She never called the cops. Occasionally, she'd swing back just to let him know who wore the pants. They were his khakis, but she wore them — stiffly starched and creased down.

(HERB ALPERT & TIJUANA BRASS, *A TASTE OF HONEY*)

I'd take the bus and escape to Hollywood, spending my allowance at Wallach's Music City on Sunset Blvd. They had fab listening booths to sample the latest releases.

(CARPENTERS, *YESTERDAY ONCE MORE*)

During the week, I'd check the trades to find out if any A&M artists were making personal appearances.

(CHRIS MONTEZ, *CALL ME*)

He holds the Montez LP.

The first time I heard "Call Me," I thought it was a fish — that's what we called girls then.

When I saw Chris Montez do a local TV Dance Party on KRLA, I couldn't believe this pretty boy CHOLO was a SINGER with a number one hit.

Weeks later, on Boss Radio, Chris did a call-in promo.

(CHRIS MONTEZ RADIO MESSAGE)

Did you hear that? Flawless Spanish! A first on Top 40 airwaves. I felt something come over me, something I had never felt before. Blame it on my youth, but Chris taught me that a young Latino could have dreams. He became my guide to a world I never could have imagined. My hero.

But then, my "supposed Latin temper" flared up, when the radio "diss" jockey called Chris "Miss Montez" over the air!

I had to defend him. Scared stiff, I nevertheless called in:

 "Chris has more hits than you have listeners. He headlined the Beatles European tour, and you question his manhood?"

There was silence on the other end of the line, *pero estaba encabronado*, I boldly ventured where no other Mexican had dared.

"Then you confuse him with Maria Montez, the Technicolor Queen, by calling him 'Miss.'

We Latinos know where you live."

Before I could do a bit from "Cobra Woman," the jerk-off hanged up—but I'll do it for you.

(aping Maria Montez) "Lay-dees! Giff me dat cobarah yule!"—and I didn't mean Xmas.

WARREN removes makeup, reveals a 40 year-old man.

I invited Tía y Tío to my debut in *The King and I*. Tía looked like a real glamour puss. Even the King was impressed. I had a crush on him already.

Auntie cooed about how handsome I looked and how she had wagered Irv that I'd make it "in the biz."

She knew I was gay from the moment I lip-synced BOTH Karen AND Richard Carpenter.

He holds up the Now & Then *LP.*

Talk about an early gender illusionist!

(CARPENTERS, *ONE FINE DAY*)

Afterward, Irv paid me the supreme compliment.

"The best thing about your drag was that you didn't lose your masculinity in it."

I identified with the Carpenters. They had left Downey just down the road from Whittier and never turned back. Ditto, little me.

Tía Luisa convinced the Larry Parkman Agency to represent me. She also handed Mom a cashier's check to cover incidentals.

"Hijo, you know $500 is a lot of moolah. I'll help if you do your part."

How macha — macha do about nothing!

The agency submitted me for a Disney feature: "Toby Tyler at the Circus." Off we went to Hollywood. Mom drove her battered pickup just like Mercedes McCambridge in *Giant*. Oh Mary, it was better than a trip to Frontierland.

Slides of traveling on the Hollywood Freeway.

BLACKOUT

ACT ONE, SCENE TWO

WARREN: I learned about the casting couch in one EASY lesson. The director—a cockeyed New Zealander—had me read a scene while he sat behind his desk rifling through his drawers!

When Toby Tyler says, "I'll join the circus and ride elephants and camels," I sang in my best Betty Hutton voice while humping an imaginary elephant:

"Cum to da Circus, the Gray-tist Show on Earth."

Mister Kiwi wasn't even listening. Instead, he stood up and shot his wad on my smiling 8 x 10. I was pissed.

How dare you spit on my picture. My mother paid $50 for these, you—

I was at a rare loss for words. As he zipped his trousers, I laughed out loud.

My dog has a bigger dick than you and slammed the door in his friggin' face.

On the way home, in tears, I told Mom about Mister Kiwi's *petite debilité*. She was fit to be tied. She blamed me.

"Look at me when I'm talking to you—*Maricón*!"

Wiping tears, I glimpsed a marquee: *King of Kings* with Jeffrey Hunter.

"Mom, let's see a movie."

Without another word, she bounced over the cattle guards—speed bumps to you city girls—for the next exit.

Bad choice.

(MIGUEL RIOS, *A SONG OF JOY*)

> Afterward, she ranted about how Jesus made his mother proud by dying on the cross. I was too young to die although with longer hair, I might have fit the bill.
>
> At home, I caught her off-guard by quoting the pubescent Jesus: "*Oy vey*, I must be about my father's business."
>
> She broke into tears. I was a wicked Babylon Baby for doing that, but I felt as spotless as a lamb.
>
> "Howsoever thou pursues this act, taint not thy mind, nor let thy soul contrive against thy mother aught; leave her to heaven, and to those thorns that in her bosom lodge to prick and sting her."

(CHRIS MONTEZ, *THE LOOK OF LOVE*)

> Wouldn't you know it? Tía returned from New York City raving about *The Boys in the Band*, the first openly gay hit play written by Mart Crowley, Natalie Wood's male secretary.
>
> I had the original cast double disk LP on A&M.
>
> *Shows* The Boys in the Band *LP.*
>
> Of all its characters, I bonded with—
>
> (zeros in on the album's cover)
>
> —Emory! I used his most fabulous line as my personal mantra and to welcome Tía home.

(THE BOYS IN THE BAND, *ORIGINAL CAST*)

> (as Emory) "Oh Mary, it takes a fairy to make something pretty."
>
> Well, Tía had her own surprise—a new job as a real estate agent to the stars in Hollywood.

Even more astounding, she had left Irv—for a woman!

Mom who was five minutes and three seconds older than her twin sister wasn't amused.

"Why don't you just move in with her—him," she growled.

Tía grabbed me and off we went in her Cadillac El Dorado just like the Carpenters leaving Downey.

(CARPENTERS, *FUN, FUN, FUN*)

The times they were a-changing for us Latinos: The East LA Blowouts, Cannibal and the Head Hunters, the Chicano Moratorium, Santana, Chicano poetry, the killing of Ruben Salazar.

And, if that weren't enough, a disproportionate number of Raza *soldados* were returning home from the Vietnam War in flag-shrouded caskets.

I tried to join Mexican American youth groups like MAYO y MECHA—even the Brown Berets.

(CAT STEVENS, *PEACE TRAIN*)

But when I asked for solidarity with valiant Latina drag queen Sylvia Ray Rivera, who had confronted the pigs at Stonewall, I was taunted.

Los pinche machistas responded just as Black Panther Eldridge Cleaver did when asked about the role of women in the revolutionary struggle:

"The only position for fags and bitches in the movement is horizontal."

I was an outcast. I dyed my hair and changed my name from Amado Guerrero Paz to the radical WARREN PEACE.

At Hollywood High, I met other kids like me. Before long, we were skipping classes and hustling from the steps of the Selma Avenue Baptist Church half a block away.

(SERGIO MENDEZ & BRASIL 66, *FOOL ON THE HILL*)

My first client was an aging TV band leader who wanted to do it on a trampoline—ah, one and ah, two and ah, whoop-ee!

Remember the TV star that used to make a grand entrance every week in a stunning gown? Well, one night her not too *young* son picked me up. Alas, poor Yorick, he turned out to be less than dazzling.

(HERB ALPERT, *THIS GUY'S IN LOVE WITH YOU*)

I fell in love. Valentin was his name or Val VERGA as I later nicknamed him. He was the first REAL Latino I found simpatico. A Mexican national, he spoke as much English as I did Spanish. Yet something clicked.

We met in the washroom of the Gold Cup on Hollywood Blvd. I was sighing with relief when his voice came out of nowhere.

"Are jew de famoso singer Antonio de Jesus que my sister adore?"

Was he doing speed? Was I?

I shook my head no. Although I was once mistaken for Maria Conchita Alonso—in a certain light.

But he stood there holding a paper towel and a pen. I signed it: Warren Peace.

"*Jijole!* You're not Antonio. But, if you be *famoso* someday, I have *un autógrafo* already."

I fell for him like a ton of bricks. I invited him to my window table at the Cup where I had been holding court with a potential sugar daddy—whom I immediately dismissed.

Val went to the jukebox and punched in what became our song.

(CAROLE KING, *IT'S TOO LATE*)

In the seedy Hotel St. Moritz on Sunset where Judy Garland once slept, Val swore if he didn't make it big in this town, he'd jump off the Hollywood sign.

Instead, he got into porn.

(MARIA CONCHITA ALONSO, *LA LOCA*)

"They pay me a THOUSAND dollars to do a Porno. *Tengo que hacerlo para mi familia.*"

Can I be your co-star?

"It's a snuff film. I shove a razor sharp dildo up some asshole's ass and jack off as he bleeds to death."

Silly me, so fucking dense.

"If anything goes wrong, swear to send *el dinero* to my Santa Madre."

What could go wrong?

"Me pueden matar!"

(JOE COCKER, *YOU ARE SO BEAUTIFUL*)

I never saw Val alive again. I first heard the buzz in the clubs: The police found a severed head in a dumpster in an alley behind Santa Monica Blvd.

I called a Hollywood vice squad sergeant who was into rimming. I agreed to try and identify the head.

(PROCOL HARUM, *CONQUISTADOR*)

>*WARREN holds the plastic-wrapped head.*

>There was a look of wonder and surprise on his face. They couldn't close the eyes. He looked so handsome—like Valentino in a silent film sensing his beloved in danger. He'd ride to save the day.

>I asked the sergeant for a police mug of the head. Long story short, I got the head shot.

(HUMBLE PIE, *I DON'T NEED NO DOCTOR*)

>*WARREN slam-dances, attempting to blot out what he has just recounted.*

(THE FLYING BURRITO BROS., *SIN CITY*)

>*WARREN hitchhiking/hustling.*

>*DJ moves downstage on skateboard, turns a trick, gives Warren a cocky thumbs up. He freezes as Warren speaks.*

>What was that? Was he mocking me, my middle age? My paunch?

>*WARREN circles DJ and inspects him as he would a sculpture on exhibit.*

>*He stares into DJ's eyes.*

>What the fuck?

(SHERYL CROW, *ALL I WANNA DO*)

>*WARREN grabs DJ from behind in a wrestling hold. He whispers in DJ's ear. DJ mouths Warren's words as a young man.*

WARREN: I'd go to the Odyssey on La Cienega Boulevard.

DJ: We couldn't get in until after hours when they didn't serve liquor, but the drugs were everywhere. Chicken hawk VIPs would look us over like a fast food menu: southern fried, tender strips, regular recipe or *pollo loco*.

WARREN: Arthur J's on Highland became the new hustling Mecca days after *Time* did a cover story on homos.

DJ: Selma Avenue and Yucca were abandoned for Santa Monica Blvd., an ugly zigzag of telephone poles and jagged wires crisscrossing over streetcar tracks.

He squeezes DJ's nipples.

Thirty bucks was the going rate. Men of color rarely ventured into white trash turf. I was native born and bred, so I squeezed in.

WARREN: I became a specter on the Sunset Strip — an Anglophile worming my way backstage in search of uncut blokes.

Warren releases DJ from his choke hold.

Frampton came alive! So did I!

He throws a Peter Frampton album at DJ.

Confused, DJ takes the LP and goes upstage to booth.

It happened in the men's room. I was pissing, again.

A cute Brit like a long-haired Herman of Herman's Hermits paraded up to the urinal. He flopped a nice size dong, farting as he pissed.

"How's it hanging, Chief?"

Warren mouths "Peter Frampton" to the audience.

He barely noticed my bugged-eyed expression as he zipped and departed.

I-DJ

(PETER FRAMPTON, *I'M IN YOU*)

> *Warren strokes and caresses himself to the music. Turns away as if to climax.*
>
> *His head is turned back.*
>
> And if! I didn't come—
>
> (singing)—"It's not cause I couldn't, it's not cause I wouldn't, and you know, it's not cause I shouldn't, it's simply because"—
>
> *He turns menacingly to AUDIENCE.*
>
> —You couldn't fucking make me!
>
> I moved on to harder core. At Rodney Bingenheimer's English Disco—Snort? One line or two?—I blew the bass player for Humble Pie.
>
> *Gets off his knees, staggering.*

(THE TUBES, *WHITE PUNKS ON DOPE*)

> It ended at a Tubes concert. By then, I'd slipped from bleeding limeys to any hard rock cock. I got zonked on bad meth at the Greek and lost my way in Griffith Park.
>
> "What's your name? Is it Mary or Sue?" A park ranger sang.
>
> "I'm trying to find the Hollywood sign so I can jump off."
>
> He notified EMS and they called my folks from Queen of Angels.
>
> I remember mama standing over me shaking her head as if I was the worst investment in her thirty-year marriage.
>
> In my dementia, her stylish Afro-Puffs became earphones.
>
> "Oh, let me listen."

She fell over me. "What have they done to my baby?"

(THE POLICE, *KING OF PAIN*)

During my recovery, my father and I bonded.

He'd come into the kitchen, drinking his usual cold one, chomping on a burrito, as we'd talk.

Once, he wondered why I identified as a Chicano.

"You were born in Whittier, Amado, *¿Porque dices que eres de Chicago?*"

He laughed at his *faux pas*. Believe it or not, that was the closest moment I ever had with my *jefito*.

Weeks later, I asked Mom why Dad had stopped visiting. She blanched. He had died in a car accident, coming home from a bar, months before my breakdown.

I had been rattling on with a ghost that entire time! Had it been the peyote? Or were Latinos imbued with the power of magic realism after four hundred years of solitude?

I learned the loving tongue of español and the defensive art of tae kwon do. I began to heal.

(JOAN BAEZ, *DIAMONDS AND RUST*)

WARREN moves in slo-mo martial arts fashion.

Yo Amo. Tu Amas. El Ama. Nosotros Amamos.

By now, Tía wore man drag in public. She said they were casting a feature with an all-Chicano cast. Hollywood was looking for LATINS.

(HERB ALPERT, *RISE*)

She was right. I dyed my hair black and did the rounds again.

WARREN struts like a low-rider pachuco.

Not bad, eh?

It was good enough to get me a callback to test for a slim Sal Mineo type.

Off the record, a gossipy trick confided:"It's going to be an East LA gang film, sweetie."

Music out.

I was cast in *Low-rider Demons*, a quickie exploitation, even more quickly banned when gang violence broke out in the City of Angels. The media blamed it on the film.

I sent half my salary to Val's mother in Veracruz. I allowed one luxury: a mural near the alley where his body—head— was found.

WARREN removes his shirt and puts on a heavy orange car coat.

(PETER FRAMPTON, *SHOW ME THE WAY*)

In La-La Land, there is no such thing as bad press. With the gang film in the news, I was sent on a one-day promotional junket to Noo Yawk City—*The David Susskind Show*.

I was virtually the only normal person on the program.

(PHIL OCHS, *OUTSIDE OF A SMALL CIRCLE OF FRIENDS*)

(holding fag a la Susskind) "Mr. Peace, Hollywood creates violence for sheer profit. Don't you find that so Biblical? So Sodom and Gomorrah?"

I felt the hot klieg lights as blood rushed to my face.

"I'm just a spic fag who got a break. You haven't even seen the film. If a black-exploitation flick causes a stir, are you going to blame the brothers for it?"

(PHIL OCHS, *OUTSIDE OF A SMALL CIRCLE OF FRIENDS*)

(stomping out cigarette) Susskind lucked out. A snowstorm caused a power outage in the studio.

Walking back to the Hotel Edison on 47th Street, retracing James Dean's steps, Times Square was a winter wonderland.

A ticker tape above me flashed: KAREN CARPENTER DEAD OF HEART FAILURE.

I fell to my knees—shattered! What the hell was I doing here?

A blinding white light suddenly enveloped me. And I heard her voice, a lilting lullaby.

(CARPENTERS, *YESTERDAY ONCE MORE*)

A forty something male: horn-rimmed glasses, roller skates, white tutu, and a black halter top—appeared in the freezing whirl. His—her boom box blasted Go-Go's as she whizzed by.

(GO-GO'S, *OUR LIPS ARE SEALED*)

WARREN opens his coat as a matador's cape.

I froze in my tracks. She circled back. Her starry wand touched my head:

"Phffft! You're a fairy."

I couldn't believe it. I had been be-KNIGHT-ed—be-FAIRY-ed.

BLACKOUT

ACT TWO, SCENE ONE

On a bare stage performing *Ham-a-lot*.

> *WARREN enters dressed half-man, half woman, much like Olivier in* The Entertainer.

> *Behind WARREN, a projection of the 1921 silent film,* Hamlet *starring Asta Nielsen as the Danish "Princess."*

WARREN: "To be or not to be: a Dane or a Dame? That is the question! Whether 'tis nobler in mind to endure the shitty masses who look askance at deviations from the norm, and cannot comprehend the peccadilloes of those who in their lives do not conform to the method of those squares who nightly would bare buck and grunt and sweat atop a frigid wife, from such calamity, Oh fates, spare me, from such a dreary life.

"Now, there's the rub!

"If I could be but transformed into a frail, wear high heel shoes and a low-cut gown and not be thrown in jail. There I could set those he-men all afire and express my lewd libido and repressed desire—to be sought instead of seeking; to be kept instead of keeping; to sit down when one is leaking—'tis a consummation devotedly to be wished.

"Oh, Denmark doctors, quacks and proctors, make me a dizzy dame not a melancholy Dane.

"Soft, you now, the fair Christine, Jorgensen by name, wanders on thy orisons. Be all my sins remembered, and all my fears dismembered."

(singing) "Oh, Something's rocking in Denmark, and it might as well be me. Have a Danish doc change my sex from he to she. Whoopie!"

Spot out. WARREN exits.

ACT TWO, SCENE TWO

Backstage at the Pair-A-Dice Ballroom.

Lights in DJ booth begin to pulsate.

(JUNIOR VASQUEZ, *IF MADONNA CALLS*)

DJ dances to the music.

WARREN enters. He moves to the DJ booth. He unceremoniously removes the disk playing.

WARREN: Geez, Louise!

(CHAS JANKEL, *GLAD TO KNOW YOU*)

(to DJ) That snowstorm became a blizzard.

I was stuck in the city for a week.

To wile away the time, I headed to those legendary record shops in the Village—from Bleecker Bob's to Second Coming. I was in vinyl Valhalla.

By then DISCO was DOA and in its place a new style of dance music was slouching into the dance clubs to be born.

I soon learned that nothing compared to the creative edge of a LIVE mix-master. I was smitten. Moving to the narcotic beat, I felt connected.

I set out to find the clubs that played this new mutation.

The Paradise Garage was the first—a gay Willie Wonka chocolate dance factory. DJ Larry Levan was the main man. He made magic with the music—and cast its spell onto the dance floor.

(TAANA GARDNER, *HEARTBEAT*—*Club Version*)

Next, Jellybean Benitez at the Fun House. The Puerto Rican DJ with a wicked beat later made his GF Madonna into the reigning dance club queen.

(AFRIKA BAMBAATAA, *PLANET ROCK*—Jellybean Remix)

Club DJs were creating an ambiance that I had never experienced. Lightning struck: The DJ was god of this new groove nation.

DJ breakdances to the music.

My heart was pumping. I wanted to storm the DJ booth and give it a go like the first time I learned to spin a top, to ride a bike, to feel the power, to inspire others to believe.

(MALCOLM MCLAREN, *BUFFALO GALS*)

DJ uses a jump rope to double-dutch.

And suddenly, a true believer appeared.

"You're my HERO." He said. "I love the way you socked it to Susskind. Mama and I kept shouting, 'Right On, Brother Peace.'"

In the din, I learned he was Kevin Smartt with two T's, Harvard, class of '78.

An ethnomusicologist, Kevin had a Ford Foundation grant to research a book on white West Coast jazz. He vowed to call me once he moved West. I was doubtful and figured he was another smooth operator out for a one night stand.

When I returned to California, I couldn't get an acting job to save my ass. Irv—Tía's ex—tried to comfort me:

"You never were an actor. You're a personality."

Well, I had personality, yet I always fancied myself an entertainer.

True to his word, Kevin came out West and jump-started my love life. His research would keep him in the Southland for a year or more. He liked the weather—and loved California men.

We reconnected at Black and White night at Studio One. He drove me to his loft near the old Rudy Vallee mansion in the Hollywood Hills. He asked me to move in. I did.

We had sex of the highest order. His cock was so baroque with a Michelangelo spiral to it. Oh god, it was the screw of Archimedes. His balls just hung there so low and full.

(frustrated) I can't get too worked up telling circle jerk stories.

We also became business partners. We opened Vinyl Vit-ah—phone, a used record storefront on Melrose Avenue near Fairfax High, whose most illustrious alumna was music mogul Herb Alpert.

Speaking of Señor Simpatico, his new boutique Spanish language label, Discos A y M, had signed Miss, oops, Chris Montez to croon en español as well as that cute—

He removes a poster from a record album and unfolds it.

Antonio de Jesus—whom Val had adored.

(ANTONIO DE JESUS, *SIGUEME*)

Months later, a sleaze bag came into the store, desperately seeking a dance jockey for the Pair-A-Dice Ballroom. I jumped at the opportunity. My ticket to ride?

WARREN opens his bag, gloating.

Pure virgin vinyl!—Not that plastic CD crap.

(CEE CEE PENISTON, *FINALLY*)

WARREN and DJ dance with abandon.

The first night at the Pair-A-Dice was apotheosis. Hundreds of men stripped to the waist dancing to the tribal beat.

A silver ball spun its fractured light over more glittering stars than even fucking M-G-M. The room reeked of gay incense amyl nitrate, poppers.

We were moving on up, just like the Jeffersons—then gay cancer struck.

Music out.

Oh, Mary, never have so many tried to unravel the mystery of what was making us sick.

Was it fisting, rimming, tainted blood, hepatitis B, poppers?

Who had poisoned our fountain of youthful indulgence?

(HUMAN LEAGUE, *DON'T YOU WANT ME*)

(cynically) Remember that one?

No one wanted to accept blame. Vicious wags blamed hustlers, the homeless, newly arrived immigrants. It was awful.

Bathhouses closed over night. The gay club scene was DOA.

They razed the gay Century Theater at Hollywood and Normandie and left a gaping hole as if a cancerous cyst had been extracted.

(PROCOL HARUM, *A SALTY DOG*)

My world was spinning off its axis. I had to reconnect—ground myself with my *raices*.

He touches his blond fuzz.

Well, not those roots—

He starts to unbutton his jeans.

—Nor those.

I mean *mi cultura.*

In 1985, a momentous event provided the perfect vehicle.

Over 50—count them and weep—Latino music legends gathered at the A&M Studios in the heart of Hollywood to record a charity single *en español* to aid starving children in Latin America.

The idea wasn't original—"We Are the World" had been recorded at A&M months earlier—but the cause was noble.

(to DJ) Ah-ahem!

WARREN signals the booth. DJ has missed his sound cue.

Well, we're waiting. Are you playing with yourself?

I got into the historic recording session by a fluke. I was standing outside the studios, when some gofer handed me these cue cards—I was to alert the sound booth as to who sang next.

(HERMANOS, *CANTARÉ, CANTARÁS*)

Boy, if my *jefito* could see me now.

WARREN flips through cards until he reaches the name of MENUDO.

The music stops.

I haven't even gotten to Apollonia or Vikki Carr yet. And one of them will surely be at tonight's show.

DJ exits.

This recording is heaven sent to open tonight's show and resuscitate this old puppy.

I'll make a comeback before I'm out the door. I'll stay all night and do all 50—well, the A&M artists—although Sergio Mendez and Brasil 66 might be a bit daunting.

I never wanna go home, I never—(to DJ)

—What! It isn't an A&M recording? You're daft, punk!

WARREN in a panic looks for the label.

(to Audience) See!—The B-Side has a Herb Alpert cut! I am vindicated!!

There is no A&M label! The fucker was released by—close your ears and think of John Cage—(gasp) CBS Columbia.

(to DJ) Nice work, Sherlock. Just for that, you get two extra points. But don't think you can be rude and escape censure—minus two points for insolence!!

Now, where was I?

Some executive bilked the funds for the Feed *Los Niños* Charitable Foundation. The starving urchins in Bogotá, Tegucigalpa and San Salvador never saw a single peso.

Their grandchildren are the ones in need of relief now.

So much for this prodigal son's return trip to AZTLÁN.

WARREN puts a black silk slip over his tights and wraps a towel around his head.

I met Val's fave Antonio de Jesus who afterwards signed an album for him. Somehow, my fractured Spanglish didn't communicate clearly that Val was dead.

As he looks in his dresser mirror, he uses the Antonio de Jesus album to cover his own face.

(reading) "Para Valentin—tu estas en mi, yo estoy en ti, amigos siempre, Antonio."

Poor Toño, guess, he tweaked on Peter Frampton lyrics to write anything original.

Well, who needs this fodder anymore? Who even remembers? Who?

He throws the album into a wastebasket.

A shocked DJ quickly retrieves it.

(lighting a votive candle) "For 'tis better to be that which you destroy than by destruction dwell in doubtful joy."

It's impossible to do a good Judith Anderson. She's impossible!

What's worse than a queen doing a bad Lady Macbeth?

Why a bad Ophelia.

(BARRY DE VORZON, *NADIA'S THEME*)

I met Felice shortly after my failed movie career. From behind, she looked like Luis Miguel when he looked like Jodie Foster.

I couldn't keep my eyes off her bubble butt ass.

She noticed me noticing her. Finally, she swaggered up.

"Say War, let's make love. If it's a girl, Venus, if it's a boy, Mars. Wanna boogie?"

(JOE JACKSON, *IS SHE REALLY GOING OUT WITH HIM?*)

Didn't I tell her that *moi* was tres gay? *Plus certainement!*

(with brogue) "We are errant knaves all. Believe none of us. Go thy ways to a nunnery."

She retorted."I'm perfectly aware of that bloody misfortune. Nobody's perfect."

Finally, she just moved in. I was still involved with Kevin.

Shrugs.

She was a punk Veronica Lake without the peek-a-boo. Don't remember Veronica? Rent *Sullivan's Travels*. I'm no Fatty and Sissy. I mean Siskel and Ebert. But I give it two thumbs up the kazoo.

(SUZANNE VEGA/DNA, *TOM'S DINER*)

After returning from a club date in San Diego, I found a rain-stained message from Felice.

She was going to Vancouver—pregnant with twins?

I never saw her again. Had she been abducted to bear children in an alien nation? Are there two Czech-Mex half-breeds dancing somewhere to a new world beat?

WARREN sings STING a cappella.

(STING, *I'M SO HAPPY, I CAN'T STOP CRYING*)

I was in such demand to do theme shows throughout Southern Cal that I stopped going to the record store.

Kevin flew to New York to see his publisher over the cover for his jazz book.

WARREN Removes slip and T-shirt.

I started classes in Zen Buddhism.

No, not the OOOMM incense in the temple but the shaven head, Zen Koan variety, a latter day Guadabuddhist if you will.

My first Koan was the deepest: "Grandfather dies, father dies, son dies—this is good fortune."

Fucking Heavy Shit, verdad?

(ANNABEL LAMB, *RIDERS ON THE STORM*)

I was still contemplating that one as I skated from Scandals the nightclub on La Brea at four AM. I was pretty high—not from pharmaceuticals but from sheer adrenaline.

As I paused for a traffic light, some Cholos in an old Chevy whistled. I ignored them until the drunken slurs started:

"PUTO" and "MAMA VERGAS."

A beer bottle hit the curb. I skated faster.

The area around Las Palmas Avenue was a DMZ. A bottle grazed my head. Bleeding, I skated to an all-night convenience store. Closed. Next door, a flea bag hotel sign blinked: OTEL—Oh, tell.

I veered on Yucca toward Highland. A crack in the sidewalk, crack, crack, break your mother's back.

I fell on my fucking face in front of Patsy D'Amore's, the shuttered restaurant where James Dean and Elvis partied.

I tried to catch my breath and stared at the empty lot where Trader Vic's once stood. This was the street where I had hustled, where I had met Val. The boulevard of broken dreams—and now broken noses.

The Chevy Impala returned, dropped off two guys, and sped off.

"Watch if anyone's coming, ese."

"No, please don't hurt me. I wasn't doing anything."

I was acting like a complete sissy. Why?

WARREN *assumes a tae kwon do position but slips.*

One of the guys wiped my face with his hands.

"See. I told you! It's him! The *puto* from that bootleg video, *Low-rider Demons.*"

If you want a copy or an autograph just ask, bro.

"*Chale!* We want *panocha*, pussy!"

Oh God, they're going to fuck me and then kill me. I tried to yell but gagged on my blood.

The drunker guy locked me in a mock embrace.

"You're cuter than those *putas* in TJ."

The Judas gave me a French kiss. Coming up for air, he let out a bloodcurdling Jorge Negrete yell. *Ájua!* He shoved his hairy crotch in my bleeding face.

"*Mama, Puta!*"

Flash. He couldn't keep a hard. My warm-ups were down to my ankles. Someone yelled, "Shut the fuck up" as a fat candy cane penetrated my ass.

The *cabrones* didn't have the balls to use their dicks.

A Polaroid Flash. Another pulled my head UP by my hair and rode me.

Flash. Pop. Bang. Impaled at both ends.

(hallucinating) A patrol car siren blasted down Hollywood Blvd. The start of the Christmas parade? I was fading.

Was the grand marshal float first or last? Why couldn't I remember? The crowd roared. I saw them! The Carpenters.

(gagging) Karen and Richard would save me. They tossed confetti.

"Have a merry Xmas, Mary!"

WARREN collapses.

(CARPENTERS, *CALLING OCCUPANTS OF INTERPLANETARY CRAFT*)

DJ rushes from the booth and holds WARREN. He helps him into a wheelchair.

I required a MAJOR overhaul.

DJ: A concussion.

WARREN: A ruptured spleen.

DJ: A severed tongue.

WARREN: A broken nose. I was out of commission six months!

DJ: Two years!

WARREN (in chair, irate) "Do you want to press charges?"

> (interrogated, scared) "No! I didn't proposition those boys."

> "Yes, I was arrested for male prostitution as Amado Guerrero Paz."

DJ: As John Doe.

DJ returns to the booth as Warren moves downstage.

WARREN: I never heard if those "kids" did time. Then a letter arrived from Chino, where one of my "co-stars" was incarcerated for narcotics possession.

In his curlicue handwriting, my fan wondered if I might have the Polaroid from that night. He signed it, "Shy Boy Valdez. C/S."

I framed his missive in my DJ booth like those you see in liquor stores. My first buck: a three-dollar bill.

I was still too weak to return to work. I tired easily. Any colds or high fever and I worried myself sick. No sex.

My partner Kevin was having anonymous sex at the peeps.

Francois—no "e"—Sagan, a wealthy frog prince, bought the Pair-A-Dice and asked me to restore it to its former glory.

"Your saving grace, War-wren, is that you realize that only *ze musique* is important, and the rest is *merde*.

Gauloises?"

He put in a *pied-à-terre*. I moved in: Le Fantôme du le Paradis!

(CEE CEE PENISTON, *MOVIN' ON*)

DJ and WARREN dancing, change places. They strip to the waist.

WARREN moves behind turntables and assumes his former DJ routine.

Retro & theme nights were my thing. Gay theme shows with muscle man drag and strippers were in. The club thrived.

Late to bed, later to rise, one *madrugada* as I jumped into bed, I felt something.

Another headless corpse? Uh-oh, Please, not the return of the curse of the Cobra Woman!

WARREN grabs at his throat.

(SUZANNE VEGA, *LUKA*)

I tried to find the damn light, he was gagging. He was alive.

Aha! "Blasted with Ecstacy. O woe is me…"

I gave him mouth-to-mouth, but he kept biting.

WARREN grabs him from behind in a Heimlich Maneuver.

He kept stuttering Nike and Calvin Klein mantras.

DJ: "To be or not. Just be it. Just do it!"

WARREN: Then the E-head's breathing got way serious. I made the sign of the cross and called 911. An ambulance took him to Queen of Angels.

Fade out? Not quite!

On the anniversary of River Phoenix's overdose, a marathon rave was held at an undisclosed location off-Sunset. I was invited to spin along with other club DJs.

Kevin and I arrived early. He was tweaking.

Backstage, I checked the roster. They had scheduled two DJs to compete against one another. I was scheduled to go against newcomer DJ MUTANT. WTF!

I decided to mix a cut from the Iggy Pop LP produced by David Bowie for two reasons. Both Bowie and Iggy had been flirting with the big H and perhaps I might glean a grain of wisdom in my remix.

As our names were announced, I got a loud and proud yell from the Pair-A-Dice faithful. But the crowd went crazy when Mutant and I faced-off—boxers ready to rumble.

He kept staring at me like a kid at the zoo wondering if the boa constrictor could break through the glass.

Both DJ and WARREN stand behind the turntables. They vie for the audience's favor and interrupt each other with a response.

(IGGY POP, *REAL WILD CHILD (WILD ONE)*)

VS

(SIMPLE MINDS, *DON'T YOU (FORGET ABOUT ME)*)

The buzz was that the younger, er, less inexperienced Mutant had been the most creative, while I had given the best performance.

Later at the Viper Room after party, everyone on Molly was cruising and higher than the Hollywood sign.

As I was pissing in the men's room, an old writer—William Burroughs?—paused in mid-stream and asked: "Are you a Chicano?"

I nodded yes with my cock, and he yelled out, "Que Viva La Raza." He then passed out, head first into the urinal.

It was Hunter Thompson, the man who stole his gonzo from the Brown Buffalo, Oscar Zeta Acosta.

As I zipped up, I distinctly heard Kevin's voice, coming from one of the stalls.

"You were awesome. Better than my worn-out…"

I flung the door open. There was Mister Not Too Smartt—two T's—on his knees, getting plowed by the goddamn Mutant.

Intent on not getting upset, I blindly wormed my way outside.

The fresh air cleared my lungs. I stood there for an eternity before I realized I was standing in the exact spot where River Phoenix ODed.

And then like a street corner preacher, quoting Biblical chapter and verse, I was reciting Shakespeare.

"Love is too young to know what conscience is; Yet who knows not conscience is born of love? Then, gentle cheater, urge not my amiss, Lest guilty of my faults thy sweet self prove: For, thou betraying me, I do betray my nobler part to my gross body's treason; My soul doth tell my body that he may triumph in love; flesh stays no father reason; But, rising at thy name, doth point out thee as his triumphant prize."

The Strip glowed neon. Above Tower Records: a mammoth blowup of Bryan Adams. From my perch, I glimpsed a video playing inside the store, but with the deafening street noise, the music couldn't be heard.

Then, suddenly Mutant was next to me. As I sang, he signed.

(BRYAN ADAMS, *HEAVEN*)

WARREN slowly walks away.

Lights dim.

(CHET BAKER, *LOVE FOR SALE*)

One afternoon Kevin and I drove out to Hermosa Beach in his old VW. We sat in some dark, dank club, the Lighthouse, where the infamous Chet Baker once played. Kevin had a few beers and I ordered soup.

Later, we walked out to the pier. Hugging, we stared out at the ocean. Two Vietnamese fishermen intent on hooking a fish didn't bat an eye at us. Kevin broke the silence.

"You know, I want to come back here after I've gone."

I thought it was beer talk. He was rail thin. His eyes radiated in the sunset. Then he did a funny thing. He stuck out his tongue at me.

"Stop," I told him. He wouldn't.

I stuck my tongue out at him.

"Hush," he said.

We'd often play word games. He'd say a word and I'd name a song title or lyric.

He repeated the word. "No, Hush."

I sang Billy Joe Royal's "Hush, hush, I thought I heard you calling my name now."

He hugged me tighter, crying and whispering in my ear. "You don't have it, sugar. I've got thrush on my tongue. Yours is healthy."

The big A ravaged him like wildfire, shaking him like a 6.9 off the Richter. He died two weeks later.

(THE POLICE, *EVERY BREATH YOU TAKE*)

As Warren enters the record store, DJ lip-syncs the lyrics.

There wasn't much left to sell of the store.

Kevin's family denied he had been gay or that I was the gay widower. I picked out the albums I wanted and sold the place to a pair of slackers who renamed it Black Plague.

I guess Mutant vaguely remembered me from that night he crashed into my pad on E. But more importantly, he had wanted to strut his turntable chops—he needed a job.

After Walpurgis Night at the Viper when I caught Kevin in flagrante delicto with Mutant, I realized Kevin—with a Special *K*—had set up the entire incident in order to arrange an audience with me.

Yet, that night Mutant proved his star attraction with the females as they threw their wet panties at him. And he was definitely a DJ talent on the verge—so, as they say in the biz, put the competition on your payroll. It makes you look better and bigger.

I hired him as my amanuensis, my 'understudy' if you will, my bareback—oops, 'bar-back' for you gay bar flies.

That night when I entered my studio—he had left a gift on my bed.

WARREN holds the box.

A year's supply of lubricants and gels? Anatomically correct sex toys?

NO, shades and a CD. How retro. How me!

Shades? He thought vampires were afraid of the light.

The CD? Procol Harum's *Greatest Hits* on A&M.

(PROCOL HARUM, *WHITER SHADE OF PALE*)

How the silly Billy ever hit on that one, I'll never know. But then it flashed. He was using those lyrics to TALK to me.

Warren lip-syncs to the recording.

(snapping out of his reverie) Stop the fucking music!!

(to DJ) That just won't do. That original hit was on Deram— NOT A&M. And we never, ever play CDs!

Warren takes the CD and throws it down.

DJ stalks angrily out of booth. He turns on the TV.

I-DJ

(REM, *IT'S THE END OF THE WORLD AS WE KNOW IT*)

> *Upset, DJ grabs his skateboard and sulks off-stage.*

> *As WARREN speaks, DJ sits on a street curb smoking.*

REM did four IRS albums on A&M, but not that one. Put on *Murmur*.

(to Audience) Is Miss Stipe into kiddie porn or has MTV gotten queerer?

> *As Warren turns off the music video, DJ is gone.*

(apes Brandon DeWilde) Oh, Master Deejay! Please come back.

(apes Deborah Kerr) "Years from now, when you speak of this, and I know you will, please be kind."

> *DJ returns, waiting—wanting Warren to reach out to him.*

> *WARREN stares at his own distorted reflection.*

> *DJ heads toward booth.*

Look at me when I'm talking to you! You little—(to his image in the mirror)—Faggot.

(SEX PISTOLS, *GOD SAVE THE QUEEN*)

> *Warren jolts up. He recognizes the cut. He consults his list.*

Winnah! Winner! Winnah! He's played 13 cuts on my list.

(to Audience) O ye of little faith, is your long term memory so short that you can't recall when Malcolm McLaren had the Sex Pistols sign a contract with A&M Records in front of Buckingham Palace? Even the Queen was watching through her peep hole.

Slide.

Slide appears.

Only a few copies of the first single were pressed, of which I have a mint copy in the family vault, and even though the punk band later signed with Virgin, it is a legit point.

We'll play the fucker tonight.

WARREN gives DJ a big thumbs-up.

He's a mofomixmaster; I'm into retro. I'm haute couture; he's hip-hop. I'm silver balls; he's laser beams.

In this biz, you can't have one without the other.

As Tío Irv once told me, "What would A be without M?"

The curse of the Cobra Woman? (crossing himself) Lifted and vanquished from the Queen-dom.

The records on my list? Does it matter? Find your own.

This is my fantasy. This is my life.

An alarm goes off in DJ booth.

DJ: (using vocoder) "The iron tongue of midnight hath told twelve. Lovers to bed; Tis almost fairy time."

WARREN: (Scottish brogue) "Speak the speech, I pray you, as I pronounced it to you, trippingly on the tongue. But if you mouth it, as many of your players do, I had as lief the town crier spoke my lines."

(PROCOL HARUM, *IN HELD, 'TWAS IN I*)

WARREN and DJ move in slo-mo. Warren appears in a white tutu, glittering roller skates, and glasses.

DJ bows before Warren and then kneels as a knight returned after his quest.

I-DJ

WARREN retrieves his scepter: a fairy wand. He anoints DJ with it.

With the power invested in me by Roller-Arena, I dub thee: DJ SILENCE.

"What a wounded name. Things standing thus unknown, shall live behind me!

"If thou didst ever hold me in thy heart, absent thee from felicity awhile, and in this harsh world draw thy breath in pain to tell my story."

Light fades and comes up on stage right platform.

WARREN through a megaphone.

"Ladies and Gentlemen, Sissies and Queers, Sodomite and Troglodyte.

I'm Warren Peace, the ringmaster of this three-dollar bill circus of thrills and chills for fairy one including, for your delight, cosmic kiddies, Chicano roadies, children with rude answers, kosher cooking tips, presidents of record companies, acrobatics and displays, the odd sane dog, the space cadet choir, assorted sound freaks, and all elements of truth.

The rest is DJ SILENCE!

Warren holds his megaphone a la Bryan Adams on Waking Up the Neighbours.

He freezes in silhouette.

Lights come up on stage left behind DJ in silhouette at turntable.

(FAITHLESS, *GOD IS A DJ*)

DJ signs as the vocal begins.

43

DJ: (signing) "This is my church. This is where I heal my hurt...for tonight, God is a DJ."

DJ walks from out from the shadows.

He is years older, a moustache, goatee, and a new found sense of himself.

He told everyone he was negative—He wasn't.

He suffered a massive brain aneurysm and died at Queen of Angels Hospital—the very place he took me, the night I ODed—the night a DJ saved my life.

Like so many others, who left their life's work unfinished, Warren died before he could perform his beloved *Ham-a-lot.*

But his—our A&M night was the best ever. Even though he dismissed me afterward—saying it was the best thing for my career.

Almost a decade later, his spirit still lives in this club and his name is legend. He would have been thrilled by all the new artists on A&M—The Black-Eyed Peas, The Pussy Cat Dolls, Maroon 5.

DJ pauses, overtaken by emotion.

"Now cracks a noble heart. *Buenas noches*, sweet prince, And flights of *los angeles* sing thee to thy rest!"

(JANET JACKSON, *LOVE WILL NEVER DO*)

Five-four-three-two-one.

(DJ SILENT, *A&M HITS video remix*)

As the music plays, a series of slides, disco balls, flashing lights, and videos of A&M stars appear on a big screen and monitors.

DJ is in CONTROL.

A blue spot on WARREN throbs, turning red hot, and then blinding white.

WARREN comes ALIVE.

CURTAIN

The Odyssey dance club after a fire. Photographer Leo Jarzomb.
Courtesy of the Los Angeles Public Library Photo Collection.

ABOUT THE AUTHOR

GREGG BARRIOS is an award-winning playwright, poet and journalist. His plays include *Rancho Pancho*, *I-DJ* and *A Ship of Fools*. He has received a CTG-Mark Taper Fellowship, a Ford Foundation Grant, and an Artist Foundation Grant for his theater work. He is a 2013 USC Annenberg Getty Fellow, and serves on the board of directors of the National Book Critics Circle. He was inducted into the Texas Institute of Letters this year. He is the 2015 Fall Visiting Writer at Our Lady of the Lake University.

ALSO BY GREGG BARRIOS

Rancho Pancho, a two-act play, explores the turbulent and passionate relationship between playwright Tennessee Williams and lover Pancho Rodriguez, who inspired the character of Stanley Kowalski in *A Streetcar Named Desire*.

Rancho Pancho follows their relationship from the summer of 1946 on Nantucket Island with novelist Carson McCullers to the summer of 1947 in Provincetown with director Margo Jones, aspiring actor Marlon Brando and the final break up of Williams and Rodriguez.

Available in paperback (ISBN 978-1-60182-331-1) and eBook (ISBN 978-1-60182-329-8)

Gregg Barrios' latest collection of poems *La Causa* is a fascinating interplay of the eras, voices, and regions of Aztlán, all in a simultaneous dialogue with each other. *La Causa* is an evolution in time, maturity, political sophistication, and expectation an invaluable document to any artistic or historical study of the soul of El Movimiento. The poems in this volume range from sonnets, concrete, songs, ballads, prose and narrative verse. It is a chronicle of the changes made in the aftermath of the Chicano Mexican American civil rights movement.

Available in paperback (ISBN 978-1-60182-500-1) and eBook (ISBN 978-1-60182-501-8)